KISS THE MOON....

The Woman Speaks And Gives Grace

POETRY by

VERONICA HALLISSEY

illustrated by

CLAUDIA HALLISSEY

Best Wishes –
Veronica Hallissey

ISBN 0-9703635-0-8

Some poems have been previously published: "The Homecoming" in *passages north* and in *Woman and Earth*: "Little Ballerina," "The Women," and "The Farm Woman."

Come with me, to this place I visit often, hidden behind an eyelash;

where it is Easter all the time and rebirth is not a sometime thing;

where gods cavort in joyous abandon.

Come, we dance…

The sun was bright coming in through the high windows on that first day of English Lit at the University.The professor was introducing herself to us and I don't know when my attention wavered, but when I looked down at my paper I found I had written these words,'Fear death, ahh I do because I love life so much'! I did not know where these words came from but it was an affirmation and I realized that those words had always been true. Even today there would be argument as to the source of them. My thoughts mix smoothly with what I consider a given and myself the instrument through which it comes. I know when the work is mine. I also know when a thought is inserted or given. And when one is given, there is a giver.

A leap must be taken when the truth of that statement is faced. It is the reason people go to church on Sunday or to the synagogue on their Sabbath. As a friend said to me. it is what we hope is true. Yet when faced day after day with significant events or thoughts, it is a puzzle as to why the evidence does not speak to the person. It will eventually and when it does, it will be the right time.

For me the beginning was in the classroom but took possession of a corner of my mind and stayed there while other things were happening. Though I was always alert to the thoughts that seemed to come from nowhere, there was this portion of me that tested the limits of what was my history. And then one night, while sitting at the desk I found words tumbling over themselves and when I was finished, a poem had been born. I found myself wondering exactly how this all came about. Surely I must have memorized this some long ago. But nowhere could I find this poem. And it was not the kind of work I would have done on my own. So I read it to the family and they laughed because it was comical but philosophical. And we let it go at that. Nobody of course believed me as to how it came about.

It took a letter to my mother to convince me that there was a Presence in my life. I started the letter and suddenly the words were writing themselves and the missive was one of good thinking and good psychology. And from that point on, the muses, or the Teachers as I often call them, were my companions.

There are those who say that within the layers of the human being there is knowledge and this knowledge rises when stresses demand answers or directions. This could very well be, and I would not argue this point at all. But when a grateful heart murmurs a thank you and the response in mind is you're welcome, followed by a sense of rightness and companionship and love, then one knows there is a Presence.

It has been a war of words over a lifetime. A philosophy has been hammered out and though it may not rest comfortably with organized religion, still I have woven a philosophical blanket with mended holes that has managed to keep me warm. It has taken all the years of my life and it has been a hard work. But I would not have missed a day of it.

Veronica Hallissey
May, 2000

CONTENTS

The Woman Speaks . . . On Love

Verbal Juxtaposition 9
The Resting Place 10
Handle With Care 11
The Homecoming 13
Abundance 14
Make A Place 15
Three Sons 17
The Child No More 18
Final Words 19
The Explanation 21
Four Of Us Less One 23
To The Fair Child 25
Final Voyage 26
In All Things Love Made Beautiful 28

The Woman Speaks . . . On Women and Friends

Little Ballerina 33
Waiting For Santa Claus 34
Her Advocate 35
The Women 37
The Housekeeper 38
Two Friends: The Woman And Her Cow 41
The Farm Woman 43
Midnight Excursion 45
A Good Friend 46
One Face 47
Tranquil Spirits 48

The Woman . . . Reflects

The True Man 53
The Chime Clock 54
The Act Of A Man 55
Bad Manners 56
Not To Promise 57
December Confirms The June Woman 58
A Deep Drink 59
Magic 60
King To Pauper 61
My Father's House 62
Plea Bargaining 63

The Dinner Hour 64
Croesus, My Country 66
How Hot The Night 67
Separate, If You Can 68
Where Can We Go? 69
Prophet, Rise! 70
Rapiers At The Ready 71
Should You Ask The Why And How 72
The Sculpting of Man 73
To Lift The Plough At Last 74
Too Long In The Dying 75
Small Comfort 76
The Word Is God 77
Eloquence 78
The Poet's Memories 79
Beginnings 80
Tracks 81
Moon Meeting 82
Generic Memories 83
Night Life 84
The Night Poem 85
Refuge In Dreams 86
Sometimes 87
The Sound Carries 88
Toward A Destiny 89
The Healer 90
The Autumn Night 91
Exit 92
The Final Gesture 93
Memory Quilt 94
In The Morning 95
When David Died 96

Her Teachers...Speak
Did You See? Did You See? 98
Blood Run Dry 99
To Safe Harbor And Wait 100
The Insomniac 101
Splitting Infinity 102
White Stone 103
For Now 104

THE WOMAN SPEAKS .....

.......ON LOVE ....

VERBAL JUXTAPOSITION

I speak the words, hesitantly.
And on my pauses
their meaning weighs
heavily.

You take my words
and on my pauses,
your meaning rests
on your totality.

We touch at points,
harvesting our
realities,
singularly.

Astonishing,
to see how we differ,
yet amazing,
to see the world we've created

moving magnificently.

THE RESTING PLACE

I've given you a thought
oftentimes of late
and find you
strangely silent.

You ponder the thought
and I ponder the silences.
Neither of us letting go
of the action.

Tied to each other,
we mentally spar,
dancing to music
only our ears can hear.

That is the way of marriage,
when minds mate
in the resting place

called love.

HANDLE WITH CARE

Don't step on it.
This heart I've laid
bare on the floor
of the heavens before.
The angels carefully
stepped around it.
So step carefully.

The tears fell
upon entry.
I did not understand
from where I had come back.
The lettered sign
over my heart now reads,
'handle with care,
if you break it,

consider it yours.'

THE HOMECOMING

My warm breath makes a circle of clear space
on the frosted pane. I gaze at empty horizons
willing your outline to appear
to give this day extra measure.

You move into view with water pails swinging,
from shoulders whose strength I know by heart,
with strides cleanly cutting
the knee high snow, effortlessly.

I move within the circle and my warm world,
eagerly awaiting your shout and stamp of feet
on the threshold., feeling already
your cold face along the line of my throat.
The woolen nap of your winter shirt
is rougher even than my hands.

It's been too long you say since you left.
And I laugh. Hardly time enough to clean the barn
for barely were you gone an hour.
And here already. My day has taken shape.

*****

The stamp of feet, the key turns
and the door clicks open.
My hands press the smooth fabric of your
well tailored coat and do not catch.
I take the leather briefcase from your hands
and lift my head for the homecoming.
It's been so long that you are gone, I say, and you laugh.
I've only been gone a week this time, you say.

I turn again to the window to find it frosted over.
And know that worlds have died
and been reborn in less time.

And today, another one.

ABUNDANCE

In my abundance, I come to you.
In my abundance, I love you.
This love shackles you not
nor binds you tightly in chains.
It gives you freedom to soar
where your spirit wills
and in the same abundance
finds you winging back to me.

Run quickly from a love
which possesses by need.
Its momentary satisfactions
bind you to a life of servitude.
Its very negation of freedom
murders the giver and the recipient.
Love beckons not out of desperation,
but out of abundance.
It is life, calling to life.
It is life, begetting life.

Come to me,
when in your abundance
you would find annihilation in not giving.
When in your joy of living
you would find death in not loving.
Come to me then.
For in my abundance I come to you.
In my abundance, I love you.
And in our communion,

the Spirit lives.

MAKE A PLACE

If you make a place in your heart,
I will move right in.

If you want to understand me,
then understand the mist that carries the eye
to places not on the landscape;
to scents piercing the senses
of roses blooming in December;
of pine trees snow laden in August;
of hyacinths in the dead of winter.

But you say, winter is not dead,
for it holds wood fires, steamy hams and crisp waffles.
It holds rosy faces on little children bundled
with too many sweaters under the garment
designed for none.

It holds love on the hearth, ghosted with hearts
surrounding people close.
It binds and holds and keeps cold winds
from approaching tender souls.
It heals.

And holds the roses by the fence blooming,
and children racing to make angels on clean snow
and marks the time of savoring
the long, hot summer past.

So if you know that,
let us work the work
and in the sprout of spring, give grace,
for what was ours too late
and much too soon
for this world and time.

But if you would make space in your heart,
I will move right in. Now.

THREE SONS

Bone of my bone,
blood of my blood,
born of desire
filtered through my heart.

You stand tall,
you men of proper mean,
with hearts fired
and found not wanting.

You've yielded to a sun
that has boiled your blood
and found the moons of your soul,
half frozen.

Vitality sapped,
stone cold,
you rise
resurrected and unafraid.

Bruises, welts and wounds,
seen and unseen,
are kissed
by a benevolent universe

and healed in love.

THE CHILD NO MORE

Round and round we go
on the carousel
that does not know
her own horses.
But I, the rider,
follow the leader.

I love you, Mother,
the child says.

Stark naked,
trembling in the moonlight,
shimmering in body silk,
I pray I do it right.
Lives of different genders circle me.
Their past and futures
wait in the fullness of my heart.

The child repeats,
I love you, Mother.

Carousels with painted ponies,
whirling dervishes,
and I don't even know their names.
But in the circle which is mine,
I now designate their leader.
He is Me.

Riding the darkness
that promises to swallow
the honky tonk world of neon lights,
through emotions
which litter yesterday,
hanging now tightly,
I ride the painted pony
straight to my resurrection.
Mother, I love you.

And the child is no more.

FINAL WORDS

I said,
I love you and
have always loved you.

And he said,
I know it,
but didn't know what to do
with that love.

And I said,
you didn't need to do
anything with it,
but simply know it.

And he said,
there was nothing
in my frame of reference
to understand it.

And then he said,
I know it now.

And then later, much later,
I knew that he knew

and then I told him again.

THE EXPLANATION

It was with stony disbelief
they watched
as I slowly lifted
the strands of hair
at the back of my head.
And when they blinked,
I smoothed the disarray
and said, did you see them?

I, of course,
had grown another set of eyes
on the back of my head.
But only after the children came,
of course.

The other one, in front,
I pointed out,
set between the other two like yours,
I've always had,
and thought the world did too.
It helped me to reach places
like your heart.

You always had a key to my head,
one said and I was shocked.
I did not know that I did.
I did not mean
to invade your privacy.

And another, breathless, shaken
rushed into the house one foggy night,
and said, you won't believe this!
(But I did.)
There they were on bicycles
all five abreast dressed in white.
They stayed in front of me
till I turned the car
at the corner, home.
And then they vanished! you wailed.
And I said, I know, I know,
they are your friends.

And another said,
we are the listeners.
The world does not listen
but we hear.

The raindrops speak
to the windowpanes and apologize
for clouding their vision.
And the windows say,
my eyes needed washing, anyway.
And I say,
you know, you know.

We hear the anguish
of the world in motion,
in the raucous laughter,
in words unsaid, said.
They see the world
in shades of white and black,
denying spectrums of themselves
in brilliant hue.
These souls who question us
are sight and sound
and color blind,

living in a world of no dimension.

FOUR OF US LESS ONE

We sit and we break bread,
the four of us less one.
We think of him but do not speak of him
who misses us as we miss him.

Our loss so great, the pain so blue,
we can but weep.
Yet so close we sit,
the thinnest veil between us,
the four of us less one.

We are who we are,
created by slow cooking
of heaven's desire for perfection
like garden vegetables, simmering.

We've come through long years of drought
with parched throats and no cold storage
for the scrubby pickings of the mind's fruit.

Now it is morning,
fresh and free of pain, newborn.
We've slept the night on buckwheat pillows.
Now the promise
that our bowls will be filled
and we will eat.

Communion at the rail on bended knee
waiting to be lifted up.

TO THE FAIR CHILD

Let me weave my dulcet magic
in and out of the strands
of your raven hair.
Within each let me weave
a strength of ten thousand
tons of steel.
Let me gift you with
a curiousity to replace
the agonies of indecision
which threaten your singular space.
And have you hanging
on the strength of a singular hair.

Take the illusion we inhabit
and circle your nimble bones
with its weight.
You will find it feather light.

It cannot be done, I hear you whisper
and I shout, not so!
I see through densities designed by mind
to have no permanent structure.
We dream and in our dreams
envision dragons,
pulling us reluctantly.

But I would take you, love,
and weave a world more permanent
than this dream. And in the magic
take refuge with old loves still new,
with images matching
the splendour of the greater self.

Use the heat of love for Earth held dear
and slay the dragon.
No use to garb in mortal strength
an illusion.
The dragon does not know

its fire is cold.

KISS THE MOON —

FINAL VOYAGE
-for my mother, Jennie

Smooth sailing, Lady,
the crew is on board
and the passengers
lining the rail for their farewells.

The Captain raises his hand
in salute
and is honored by his guard
as he walks on deck.

You, Lady,
have your anchor raised
and give the final horn
in your salute.
The flags fly high,
balloons are loosened
and you, Lady,
leave the harbor.

The final trip, the farewell voyage
is your last statement
of a life well lived,
of seas traversed
with untold stories,
of horrors and harrowing misses
of icebergs, rapids,
with the heart of you in stress
but beauty seized to breathe calm.

We negotiate the channel slowly
and answer the gun salutes
from those on shore
familiar with your passage.
Your foggy reply, a blast,
is your cry.

'Twas some journey.
But enough, for the frame weakens,
the skin stretching has begun
to show the paint peeling
and even rust pits
what has been so lovingly waxed.

Time, the elements, the exigencies
of a life take their toll.
The boiler in the heart of you
no longer has replaceable parts.
It is said, they no longer make them
to fit your model.
'Tis true.

And the likes of you
was the last from a blueprint
long ago destroyed.
Your best parts have been copied
and in the children of the mother ship
you will be mirrored.
Not the original, but more
than the original, for they will be
of their time and the best of you.

The Captain stays the watch.
You are his, his Lady.
He has gathered all that you are
and houses it in his memory.
And knows that a finer ship
will not be in the life of him.

There was only one Lady,
so strong, so graceful,
so lively and so loving.
You performed reliably
and beyond expectations.
Dry dock awaits.
But the world will feel your absence and say,

'once there was a Lady....'

IN ALL THINGS LOVE MADE BEAUTIFUL

Shedding the disconsolate membrane
from the already shredding heart,
love took a stand.
It said,'I will create'.
And it did and what was created
was a world born to glory.

In the space marking high noon,
the light was placed in accordance
to rules generated to induce order.
It rolled across paths destined for it
and the gods found that one portion
sliding further from the sun
was in darkness.

So the sister of the sun was born
and the gods called it moon.
It lighted up the dark sky, called night,
and became its own brightness.
In the shadows of the moon,
those spots light did not reach,
a life of its own arose.

In the full brightness,
love was nurtured and it flourished.
In the shadows where there was no light,
life appropriate only to shadows survived.
But it was still love, all love.

The gods walked the space, now called earth
and found it good.
So good that it tasted of salt.
So good that it tasted of fruit.
So good because love manifested itself
between them and had expression.

So good that the gods did not want to return home.
And the earth gods were born and each in turn
tightened their grip on the fruits of the earth
and lived as long as bodies dared.
They did not know that what was created
for sport of expression and learning
would become the sole reason for being.

And when they died because bodies
could no longer stand upright,
they flailed their arms.
And vowed to return again and again
and so they do.
The lines form to the right
and stretch farther than the eye can see
and longer than the heart can beat.
It continues to be so.

The doors rattled to be opened
and they open.
For humans understand the need to be born
and they favor one another
knowing that in due time,
their knock must be heard.

The taste of snow upon the tongue is tasteless
but for gods, it is the cream on skyr.
The taste of rain upon the tongue has no taste,
but for gods it is the nectar spilled on Olympus.
The sun upon the brow is warm on human skin,
but for gods it is the memory of love bestowed.

Arms tighten about the human body to signify
an Other to strengthen and to hold upright.
For gods, it is a memory, having once been held
in such a way by invisible arms,
too short now to span the space.
Moonlight once betrayed the illicit mind
gone hiking on paths best tread in daylight.
It now holds the sensual splendour for gods yearning
to recapture the memories of time past.

Hiding in the silver chalice
is the wine, nectar of the gods,
believed by earth gods to transform them.
Hiding in the bread of the peasant
is the yeast, threatening
to level the whole loaf.
And hiding within the skin of man
is the god promising to return home,

but only when he has outgrown his toys.

THE WOMAN SPEAKS .....

.......ON WOMEN AND FRIENDS

LITTLE BALLERINA

Dance for me, little girl.
Dance your dance
and show the gods
why you dance.

In the garden I see you,
toes dug into the earth,
head tilted to catch
the glint of the sun
filtering through the leaves.

You nod in assent to breezes
whispering your name.
Your lips move in intonation
of the om which separates you,
momentarily.

You pirouette perfectly,
swayed by forces
caressing you to homage
of all who you are.

I long to kneel
before the image of you.
At one with your own music,
when your arms grace sweepingly
in the silent moment,
and you take
all that is yours
and pray the garden

into a sanctuary.

WAITING FOR SANTA CLAUS

The bare floor of the landing,
midway to the top of the stairs,
began to bite her knees
and she grew weary.
Her chin pressed the ledge
of the frozen window
where her breath left a misty hole.
Her eyes followed the range
of the stars, afraid, afraid
of missing the sainted friend
who would deliver her heart's desires.

Her vigil continued and
the night grew weary of itself.
The house slept under the weight
of the wonderless slumbering within
and its old bones creaked with fatigue.

She did not move and
her eight years spoke her eight millennia.
The promise was not for now but of forever.

Erstwhile urchin, never blended the phases
of the child's dreams, but the boiling
of the witches' brew to drink
from the cauldron of life's ironies.

It was the story written of the night
in which a million stars stole the night.
She long remembered the banishment
and in her vigil, she would have
reclaimed the homestead.

It was not to be. But in its stead,
the morning fir stood
and the lights reflected the stars
which distilled their radiance
in the eyes of the child.

Not for naught was the long wait.
She claimed her right as a child of the night

and gift wrapped was her life.

HER ADVOCATE

The doctor was thoughtful as he asked, 'is she in pain?' And I said that she takes the stairs quite slowly and has difficulty in the morning. I felt as if I was describing myself. He touched her head lightly and said, 'take her home and love her.'

The walk home was longer than the other times. We talked. I told her how I knew that she hurt sometimes but together we would make it. Her head was pointed in the only direction she knew, home.

We climbed the porch and with great relief she sprawled. It was the only place in memory to put its square arms about her and say, 'welcome back.'

I watched her forget at times when a squirrel spirited her vision and she gave chase. A monumental effort for the enormous body collapsed and found its rest with four legs at right angles. She even thought at times she was a pup and she remembered from some distant time how she jumped straight up. Now she found her legs unsteady.

She does not whimper but takes time in stride. I prepare her supper with the crisp fatty bacon and no gourmet meal matches. I look upon my cereal bowl and wonder.

One voice says, 'put her out of her misery'. Another voice demands, 'would you do as much for me?' Another counters, 'what will you do with me?'

My bones become brittle now and I find rest at the top of the stairs. My eyes grow dim and I tire. Occasionally I do my spirited dance, remembered. And then my limbs remind me again that to dislodge hidden memories brings pain.

And I wonder again.

Who will be my advocate?

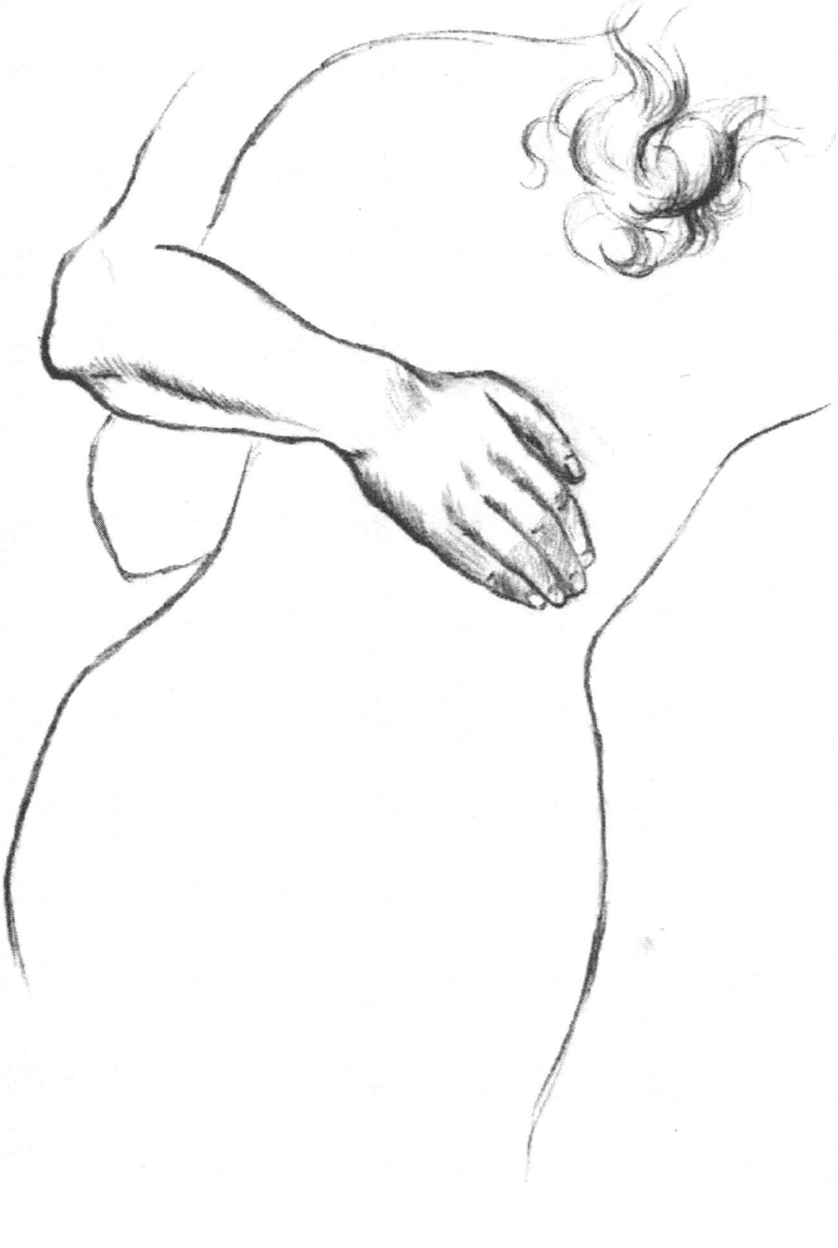

THE WOMEN

I take her hands
and the calloused palms
speak to me of work
which would find balk
at the shoes of a million mules.

She greets the guests
as mistress of the manor
and grasps the outstretched male hands
softer than her own.
They do not pass her notice.
Tears glisten in eyes so brightly held
and she does not flinch.

I remembered other hands
as rough as hers from another time.
But things have changed, have they not?
No more do my sisters carry babies
from winter to spring, from winter to spring.

Now rising from fires long dead,
a daughter, akin to the Phoenix.
With silken skin dressing the grip of a vise,
her hand takes mine.
I know where stands her mother.
I hear them speak in an embrace
that pours the gratitude
from one into the other.
I ache with what I hear;
fearing to invade their privacy
I think and yet find I cannot pull away.
In the fullness of the hour I am included.

For this the older woman labored,
from winter to spring, from winter to spring,
to borne such a one.
It is not every woman's knowledge,
but when tears mingle
in eyes beneath our knowing and hands touch
in the space above our touching,
we do not forget.

And my remembering, remembers.

THE HOUSEKEEPER

There bellows a wind
around the turrets
of the mind's house,
ripping under gutters,
sweeping under eaves,
leaving no residue.

Clean, chaste
as the sweet wind,
stands she exalted.
Prudently swiping at corners
to eliminate even
the shadow of contamination
on her brother's name.

In good time,
in due time,
the world will be
swept clean
and her father's house
will sparkle.

TWO FRIENDS : THE WOMAN AND HER COW

'They insist you do not understand,'
she said, 'and I say you do.
My heart is breaking
for what it is I am about to do.'

The woman's hand went up
and traced the ears
through which they said
the animal could not hear.
She followed the lines of the mouth
and the rough tongue reached
for the reward which was not forthcoming.

She could not keep her face
from the dear and familiar one
who stood so silently in front of her.
The tears fell from her eyes
and matted the smooth coat.
She took the rope and with practiced hand
slipped it over the head of her friend.
The wind whistled through the grasses
while the sun blazed the earth dry.
The sorry sight of the two was visible to them
who stood invisible and watched.

The path they followed was worn,
much longer usually than this day.
At the cross bridge the woman did not turn,
so her friend pulled the rope to nudge her home.
The woman cried.

'You fed my babes
when there was nothing to feed them.
You could not even feed your own.
Now I take you to the man
who will do the final act
I ask of you, to continue to feed the babes.
He will deliver you to me
and the children will eat.'

'I've asked so much of you already
and now I ask once more.
Feed the children.'

The cow moved slowly,
aware of the remorse the woman felt.
Together they made the final trip.
Soothing sounds from
her friend's attentiveness
could not alleviate the woman's misery.
'I ask of you the final favor,
feed my children.'

They wound down the path
to the waiting man and the woman
turned over the rope to him.
With swiftness she embraced the cow.
She turned abruptly. The gesture
seemed strange with no words spoken,
but more the woman could not do.
She had asked the final favor
and knew her friend did not refuse.
Their paths, well worn, had twined,
pitting the shoes of both. The bond was forged
when consciousness was attained.

The woman had held the head of her friend,
when labor threatened to take her calf
and then held the stillborn when it did.
'I understand,' she had murmured
when the night's darkness held no crying mews.
She had held the crooked pan of water
for the long drink which would never satiate
the deep thirst. She stayed the night.
In reverence she drew the colostrum
and tipped the pail onto the ground.
She could not do otherwise.

The man returned the marbled meat
the following day. He tipped
his sweat rimmed cap to bid the day.
No words were uttered.
With eyes steadfastly holding his,
she softly spoke the silence.

'The children will eat.'

THE FARM WOMAN

Woman of the Earth,
you are loved.
You gather the fruits
of your labors to your bosom
and feed the children.

You've inched your way
along the dusty path
with back bent in great fatigue
and cultivated the rows
yielding wise fruit.

You would feed out of your mouth,
those you think hungry
and then beyond measure.
The fruits are the heart
of your labors, the harvest of your
mind's philosophy,
spilling indiscriminately.

Who is left to feed you, farm woman?
What commissary is left open
to feed your hungry soul after hours?
What bookstall will house the words
between stiff covers
to increase your harvest?

Labor, till the sun
closes its blinds on the day.
Restless legs will
speed you through the night

to find the bins ever full.

MIDNIGHT EXCURSION

I saw them,
leaning against the rail
with grey curls circling their faces.
They were in animated conversation.
Their eyes were glued
to the waters, I think.
The wind blew their housedresses
about their knees.
Frowns and furrows
made ridges on their foreheads.
They jiggled with laughter.

Not out of the ordinary, you say.
Certainly a commonplace happening.
The hazy sun was evident,
but most of the surroundings, blurred.

I could have stepped
into their conversation.
They would have welcomed me.
But I did not.

It was with a start
that I realized I was the visitor.
The midnight excursion
placed me in their time.
I had broken stride

and found me another world.

A GOOD FRIEND

You stayed the night
while I lumbered my body
through a partition
closing me from life.

While I fought
through a sea of memories
holding me hostage
to long and lonely years.

You saw me
through eyes of tears
reflecting the hardness
mine needed to smelt
with coals being fired
in a heart of no use.

But you stayed,
close as my skin
and had you pulled away
I would have understood.
You stalk me yet
and I stand.

My eyes have shed
their steel casings,
now ground as dust beneath my heel.
I look inward to softer places
and find the world not so hard.

You tell me
you need to stay close
because you wish to claim
my strength if only by association,
but I ask,

of what heavenly use is a soft shell crab?

ONE FACE

She touches fingertips to a face
as lightly as a kiss of wind
and nudges memories,
clad in illusion, tentatively.

Star shaped, diamond chips,
melting snow on little faces;
nature has painted her red roses
on milk cheeks
and has buried memories
to be awakened at another time.

Everlasting memories,
but we carry the one face
of the one child

forever.

TRANQUIL SPIRIT

'He said he would always love me,
I remember that,
but he didn't, of course.'
The sister rasped her story
in between sobs
that racked her body.
She was now alone,
abandoned and destitute.

I am not certain
of whom she spoke,
her father, her husband or her God.

Another tight lipped
whispered her ordeal,
barely audible.
'I could not cope,' she said,
and the harder I tried,
the harder I prayed
and then no one came home.
They said I did not
even cast a shadow.
That was because
they stopped looking at me.'

And another bit her lips and said,
'God needed him more than I did.
He was so good, so bright.
He would have
fulfilled all promises.
I'm sure He loves him more than I could
but I loved him so much
I would have transplanted my heart.'

There was no doubt
she talked of her God.
But to whom the other spoke,
I do not know.

The black widows in their black robes
knitted their
white stiletto fingers together,
and plotted the assassination

of the Marys while they were

still in their cribs.
They could not foresee
the ruddied skins with broken capillaries
and pale hands shaking.
'Go to the closet and pray,' they were told
and of course they did.
My how they did.
They closed the door after themselves
and prayed long and hard prayers,
invoking the names of all they held dear.
And when, with parched throats,
they drank of the tranquil spirits,
they became tranquil spirits,
slow of tongue and precisely mannered.

I do not know whom they invoked,
their fathers, their husbands or their God.

They continued to be silent.
They hid their God in a bottle
among the wools that fit no longer,
stuffed their God in the knee high boots
now out of fashion.
But they would find Him again.

In a little while
when the hurt came to touch the deep
where none should touch,
when the art of coping
escaped the artist's palette,
and the shadow faded to all
but a slender hint of itself,
again they would retreat
to the closet and pray, lamenting and loud,
whimpering and afraid,
fading finally to become one
with their bottle of courage.

Cleanly washing
the mind of memories,
if just for this time,

I must cry for my own.

THE WOMAN

……REFLECTS….

THE TRUE MAN

He describes himself to me,
in fine melodious terms,
taking on dimensions of grandeur.

I smile and nod
at appropriate times,
drinking in the full tenor
of his statement.

And then he turns to grant another
his awesome presence,
while I stand perplexed, puzzled.

His words were grand
and complete his justification.
I watch in silence and
try with great effort,
to tie the man to his actions.

I would not guess they are the same.
The one I know, he told me so,
the other I know

by heart.

THE CHIME CLOCK

It is far past the hour
when the bell chimes
and I know when the hour
will strike again.

Many times we've heard
the bell strike our time
only to ignore the possibility
of a door opening.

We think it closes
forever on us,
yet the motive for its closure
is to ensure its opening.

Perhaps on a possibility
not thought of
or perhaps not ours before
this particular chime

declares us to our world and time.

THE ACT OF A MAN

It would take
a million voices
in unison
to silence the beating
of the great heart.
If then.

It would take
the laughter
of a world of children
to match the joy
harnessed by
one thoughtful act.
If then.

Then let it be written.
To ease the sorrow
of just one,
to lighten the burden
of just one,
is to be for me

the act of a god.

BAD MANNERS

It is considered bad manners
 to gloat over one's recovery
of lost fortune,
 though it was never lost
or mislaid,
 just mishandled.

In due process
 the maturation point
is toward the becoming
 of a greater something;
a no thing to be retrieved
 in retrospect.

It is a wild dashing
 toward the incarnate,
toward the ephemeral,
 toward the dislodging
of the mother lode.

In all great things,
 bad manners simply
ingratiate the human
 on all levels.
It is the identifiable
 uniting the commonality
of all men.
 It would be bad manners
to appear otherwise

 but politic to be common.

NOT TO PROMISE

'Do not look at the moon.'
she was told
'or it will spark that place
hidden from your heart
and you will mount
that one horned beast
and ride right out of memory.'

Not to resist an imperative,
she let her eyes rest
on the three quarter face
turned from her.
In her mind no words were heard
but on her face
two rivers flowed.

From the delta of her mouth
came the coarse cries
which were heard
on the other side of the moon
and the moon called the clouds
from their moorings
and bade the evening star
to kiss the orphan,
then withdrew.
The stone faced guardian

promised her nothing.

DECEMBER CONFIRMS THE JUNE WOMAN

It is June and I stand poised on the landing of the half circular staircase. I am hearing the strains of the Canon not heard in this, my lifetime. Shocked still, caught in the shadows of half remembering and yet reluctant to confront the shaded memories, I wait.

She is visible, the young woman gliding with joy to the music which carried her down the long hall. She curtsies to the throngs lining the great walls.

I stand, not moving. Her joy is mine, translating to an emptiness in my heart. The tears scald my cheeks and the rest solidify in a mass in my throat. I cannot swallow. I am in danger of drowning from within and without.

II

It is now December. I am before an ancient building in a city bearing her years gracefully. The snow is circling my feet and the wind is freezing my eyes. I am rooted to this spot. The air is ringing with the sounds of holiday; lights flicker their ritualistic colors in harmony.Yet I stand immobile.

On the second floor of the ancient building, caught in the winter of my memories, I see the long hall stretching before me. The strain and refrains of the Canon carry the young one still, waltzing yet.The violins smooth the way for her memories to be built.The red vests of the rotund violinists complement in contrast their black, slicked hair.They bend and bow in homage.Their music locks her destiny forever.

My eyes are again in danger, this time of freezing in their sockets with the salted tears that cannot stop.The memory does not move, not to one side nor the other.My will forces my eyes to play again what can only be seen in my throbbing head. Courted through centuries with great care to remain hidden, I unwittingly jarred the box housing those memories.

In retrospect, I was ready.It was my time.I turned away shaken and knowing,

the past is still happening.

A DEEP DRINK

As the evergreens drink deeply
in preparation
for the long winter,
I, too,
turn to portions of my Self
already stated and prepare.

The journey for both
is through dry country.
The oasis will not be found
except within.

I carry the water
to the evergreens
as mine, too,
is carried to me.

As I am to the evergreen,
my Self is to me,
water carriers both,

invisible to each.

MAGIC

They thought I was magic
when I kissed their wounds and
they hurt no more.
They were babes and not fully wise
to belief systems
and powers of thought as I was.

Their faith in me made them whole.
I used their belief to heal them
until one day it worked no more.

By then, they knew young bodies heal
because young bodies wish to grow old.
They also knew that what I healed
were hearts until the day my words
failed to reach their broken ones.

So they grew up and healed themselves
and I knew that my wounds would not heal
and my heart, though broken,
could not heal itself
because I was no longer young.

My body of its own accord
did not wish to grow older.
To grow older meant to hurt more.
So I did the only thing I could do.
I grew up and healed myself

and then I knew I was magic.

KING TO PAUPER

Rendering itself useless now,
the elements of Nature
first borned by Man
to work for him
have gone rabid.

But in wisdom still,
the moon continues
to pull the ocean by great force
and gently lays the rolling waves
on windswept sand,
clearing man's debris.

The wind, if amortized,
would harness its power
to push the plow.
And sun, first born of woman
would gladly warm
the earth's chilled bones
and never cast a shadow.

The earth would form
the nested nettle
where foot transgressed,
with pleasure support
the frame of man forever.

Air in bunches note
the going in and coming out of men
and upholds their stance, untiringly;
gladly yielding itself to noble ends.

Relegating himself
to the beggar's position
of that which man himself created,
the Art is lost and in its stead
small triumphs rise.
Birth and death are Nature's saviors,
preventing man

from raping her in anger.

MY FATHER'S HOUSE

I lumber about the edges of my father's house.
The corridors stretch empty before me.
Doors stand ajar, impatient for my knock.

Yet I hesitate, for I live in a familiar room,
knowing its nooks and my constructed partitions
yield only to my touch. I know too,
where the edges are not tightly sealed,
where winds sneak through
disturbing my zeitgeist.
I know at what time of day to avoid those edges.

But woolen socks do not a winter break,
nor spring tempered by autumn winds.
Here in my father's house are rooms unexplored
with answers to questions man dares not ask.

It was promised once that a room
would be prepared but went unexplained
because the question went unasked.
No one wondered how these rooms differed.

Shadows follow, casting patterns
similar to our habits, dressed in symbols
disguising our thoughts.
Furnishing the rooms will be the shapes of our days,
colored by glass prisms reflecting us.

The heart's yearning impresses the mind's eye
and doors swing wide. Worlds spills upon worlds,
breathless, intoxicating in their newness.
Yet in a moment, their familiarity is viewed
with the reaffirming recognition

of our god eyes.

PLEA BARGAINING

In the hush of this night,
let the roar in my head
lend itself with grace
to the sleeper's council.

Let them with great impunity
rest comfortably between the ledgers
of yellow sheets, decrying at once
any disturbance in the night's slumber.

I toss and turn,
stripping the nightclothes
away from my suffocating throat.
Little rest for the aegis in me.
Night school becomes a test of wills,
yet the student dare not attend.

Liberation wears many faces.
Visions at once illumine
and burden beyond measure the innocent.
Emotions torn from a psyche already battered
leaves the messenger with the message
castrated by the turn of events.

The earth's menopause
prophesies a sterile future.
The sleepers will see fit to sleep,
taking from the night
rest to determine the day's folly.
Their wax filled ears will not hear
the cry from my parched throat
as they discuss with impatience
and veiled eyes,
magic markings on the wall.

No more the dark night.
I yearn to slumber the quiet away,
reveling with the rest on stage
in complete oblivion. But,

do not take away what I have earned.

THE DINNER HOUR

"The meat loaf
is just right this time," she said.
And he said,
"the potatoes could use
a little more salt."
The knives and forks started
their upward and downward motions
and the dinner hour began.

****

The plane took off
and never did sound right.
It didn't have the steady climb
nor familiar thrust.
It banked and lost its altitude.

The bridge was full
with homeward bound.
The snow was blinding
and the roar, ominous, as vehicles
their windshields shattered, halted.
The Boeing grazed the unbelieving,
the unprepared
and went broken into icy waters.

****

The picture tube, invited guest,
sitting with the meat loaf
and the mashed potatoes,
continued its commentary.

"Isn't it awful?" she said,
with a look of pain.
And he said, "those are good pictures,"
while the upward and downward motion
of the knives and forks
kept their cadence.

The casualties mounted.
The helicopters,
their hammocks swinging,
lifted the struggling
from the cold waters.

"Oh Jesus", she said.
And he said,
"did you remember to pay
the electric bill today?"

The anchorman stumbled
over his words,
and then recovering
called in the street reporter
for an eyewitness account
of the families claiming their kin.

****

The coffee was poured.
He said,"where is the cream?"
She said,"I didn't get out today
because of the snow."

The in-the-field reporter
talked of cyanide poisoning
at the liquid disposal plant.
"It killed two of us," the spokesman said,
"and felled our fellows
as they raced to the rescue.
We don't know why it happened."

"And our in depth report
on teen age pregnancy,"
the anchorman continued,
"will be postponed until tomorrow night,
due to rapidly breaking news.
We will report on the sexually active
who won't say no and their babies.
And we'll talk of
the continuing controversy
of the advisability of sex education."

****

"Do you want dessert?" she said.
"No," he said,"I don't feel so good.
It must be something I ate."

CROESUS, MY COUNTRY

Croesus stumbled
and laid back a war torn skin
for public autopsy.

With bruises bested
by emotional welts
too deep to be visible, he wept.

In the eye of the cyclone,
the earth's erratic heartbeat
was his heart;
the blood drenching the soil
was his blood
and the screams of the mothers
came from his throat.

From Midas he inherited
his golden touch,
spewing riches tinged with decadence;
stroking the mind of man
and lulling into complacency
the aging neophyte.

Promising to pave
the illusory streets with golden bricks,
the purchase price was extracted
ounce by sweaty ounce
from the despairing brows
of the ages' overburdened.

* * * * *

We will again bathe our Croesus
in the River Pactolus.
We will anoint his open
wounded heart
with the balm of Gilead.
He will stand again
with his ancient head in the clouds
and his heart in the eye of the cyclone.
And no longer will he permit
the mothers' screams

to tear the earth apart.

HOW HOT THE NIGHT

The still air
stifles
even the act
of breathing.

The hot air
forged in the steel furnace
of daylight,
is nowhere a relief.

My eyes droop
with heat heavy
fatigue
and I take refuge

between sheets,
locked
beneath the pristine
spread all day.

My naked legs
scissor kick
in their coolness,
like swimming

in a dish of vanilla ice cream.

SEPARATE, IF YOU CAN….

Will I smell the roses
in another time,
full blown on another bush?
Will they smell as sweet?

Will I recognize the petals
as belonging to the rose,
or will I by their essences,
know them….

chaste as the morning,
a newness which speaks of rebirth,
subtle changes
requiring new form….

****

The rose will smell the rose
lingering long in the memory.
The change, imperceptible
as yours,
will be hidden in the same reality
storing the potpourri.

Until such time,
if time be weighed
and medley shaken,
spilling will be the loose petals,
a reminder of what was,
and is, still.

Will you separate yourself from the rose?

WHERE CAN WE GO?

As the sparrow falls it is noted
and the quality of life
is diminished by one.
Long ago the feathers were counted.
The color of the downy beast
was painted into the rainbow.

A child is born
in the forgotten regions
of a world too busy to take note.
The borning is observed, however,
by the cosmic populace.
Its growth watched and shepherded
and when the child cries,
the heavens lament.

There is no least in quality
or number. Each beating heart
is calculated to keep a world intact.
Each blink of an eyelid,
reason enough for the sun
to keep itself alive.

The coming together
and the going apart of each
is through a door
opening and closing
onto a portion of life, indissoluble.

Now it is here,
now gone from here,
now it is here.
Disappearing from this place,
it takes form in another.

The sparrow sings in another tree
and his song is heard
by one who left the here
and followed.

Where can we go and not be found?

PROPHET, RISE!

Now slumber the guides
who for centuries past
have given voice to what man
from everlasting to everlasting
has proclaimed;
that man immortal be.

Looking to that
which for man have been
the eternal verities,
looking perchance away
from the stillness of the hour,
to find the slumbering guides,
awakening.

Filling the eternal eternals
with that which heaven
in aeons past has filled.
Filling the empty crevasses of mind,
enslaved by those whose lust for power
is insatiable.

Arise, O Prophet!
Speak once again to ears
that yearn to hear again.
Strip the mystic veil
beclouding reality.
Unclench the fist
that grasps the temporal.

O slumbering guides, awake!
The hand is outstretched
and the mind hungers for that
which man in his finest hour

could not do alone.

RAPIERS AT THE READY

Duelists sharpen the cutter's edge
in a battle fought on grounds, ethical...
determining only
the swordsman's valor.

Languishing in corners, misted,
hidden from the probing view,
are testers, dressed in common cloth,
long seeking the true valor
in themselves undisclosed,
for proof beyond doubt
that the mystic vision
be not a dream imposed.

In a time long digested,
in a reality held valid,
in a place haunting the mind
with memories barely surfacing,
a bastion of strength struggles for place.

The duel need not a visible ground,
the swordsman need not the visible armor,
the morning need not a witching hour
to call the duelist's honor.

Required only is
the confrontation of the dream,
within the larger dream to claim validity.

The sight of choice
need only be a man's heart.
Woman has already claimed

her visions valid.

SHOULD YOU ASK THE WHY AND HOW

Should you ask and wonder,
I will tell you why and
how of everything.

The bees take their honey
with explicit direction
from the honey maker.
Liberal rules govern the process
and allows freedom
for even the most recalcitrant.
It works.

Let me answer your question
on rain and thunder.
It is the language
heaven speaks in answer
to an earth parched and
leaning toward transparency.
The heavens lament
this condition of poverty and
sheds tears destined for every inch,
then lauds its work
with kudos which rumble
in every corner.
The applause is deafening.

You wonder about the winter snows
that lace every stretch of lane,
every road, every highway,
laid with love by the handiwork
of a million angels
whose love of labor is virtuous.
Not a flake is copied
nor plagiarized by the worker
whose talent is not lost
in job description.

We make our rules to fit the game
as we play it.
And sometimes we even change them
again as we go along.
But the Master Rules do not change.
Thus it has ever been.

THE SCULPTING OF MAN

Carved light,
fading from a chiseled sky,
moans in pain
with harsh remembrances
of the child's innocence.

We take the memories
and turn with gentleness
into forgetfulness
the emblazoned cruelties,
lifting with a
scissored precision the offenses.

The light turns itself
from a day of no glory
and spitefully rubs,
with a giant's touch
a moon filled
with gold and nostrums,
to make play again
the innocence of children.

Pain shoots through
the relic's memory,
but no longer following
the tortured paths.
Instead,
in passion stilled
we see the review
of the children growing
and lose in carved light
and fading sky

the sculpting of Man.

TO LIFT THE PLOUGH AT LAST

How great and wonderful
is the borning,
the breaking of dawn
fast in the East.

How blessed is the soul
intent on magnifying its god,
borned in the heart
of many lifetimes' consciousness.

Naysaying all arguments,
lamenting all laments,
laying aside all agreements,
intent still, but weary.

It is a wondrous effort
the Great God instills in Man,
to plough the furrows of his life,

to lift the plough at last.

TOO LONG IN THE DYING

Follow me, young heart,
to places unforgettable,
amid a torrent of rain song,
amid a night of long gaiety.

Hollowed wells propound a depth
with waters clear and clean,
cups of deep to satiate thirst,
no longer to be satisfied
on this green acreage.

Hovering above this spiritual body,
is a shimmering splendour,
opening that portion of sky
which harbors ships
eager to sail away.

Loosen your grasp.
The journey is a safe one.
So soon you forget!
Lamenting a leave
from bondage too cruel
to calculate,
shadows the spirit
yearning for freedom.
Patiently, it waits,
with knowledge inborn and
truth its vesture.

The great heart is yours,
flowing with its natural boundaries,
sucking from the noble earth
its last vestige of mortality.
You've been too long in the dying.

Healing begins with time's release.

SMALL COMFORT

In waves, the moans
of the conscience stricken reached the heavens.
In waves, across the lands, reaching tidal proportions,
the laments were cradled in the clouds,
due in time to wash across the hearts of the unborn.

The cries of why? why? and why?
were epidemic as they swept the Great Mind
and lodged in its bosom.
The gods, bewildered, wondered why (themselves)
the questioning continued when in ages past
man learned so well.

But now the 'why?' from woman's lips
demanded an answer to soothe her breast
grown bloody with irritation;
a cancer eating her insides,
moving earth as well as heaven to answer.

'I said' no longer was sufficient
for the rising tide of an ego too long suppressed
and not to know its day.
No longer sufficient to walk in shadow,
when knowledge, full blown was hers.

The 'I said' no longer held terror from either God or Man.
'I said' no longer could be used
to keep suppressed the horror in the cry falling on man's ears.
The children vanished from the hearth
and woman rose, unafraid.
No more the reason of hunger or cold
from the winter's snow to cover the babes' heads,
as she found her head immune to pain inflicted
by mindless gods, both earth's and heaven's.

Too late she knew, but all in due time.
For progress, such as it was had reason to bed.
The heel must first strike the ground before the foot implants.
She did not know the muscle she had to carry life's burdens,
nor the control it required to balance it all.
Unknowingly, the ballet performance

was exquisite.

THE WORD IS GOD

In the beginning was the word
destined to touch the mind of man.
But the prevailing Spirit in its wisdom saw fit
to encumber each with the power to discern.

Meanings floated into space,
shaping themselves to fit the receiving mind.
Reaching their destination,
their shape changed to fit the owner.

Such turbulence! Such uneasiness!
Albeit because the word had taken life and risen
to meet the heart's need.
The speaker's heart had taken its intent
and placed upon the ethers the heart's desire.
It gathered cadence as it rode
to meet the receiver's prejudices.

The sender's intent lay silent, lost.
The heavens only acknowledged
its primordial meaning.
Can it be said in truth
that the word be god?
It is.
For within its power to create
it moves with desperation to voice feelings,
to give breath to visions and to heal.

The word created creatures and dynasties,
wars and rebellions, held peace in abeyance
and brought us to life.

So speak softly when speaking.
Words carry the weight of the heart
with intent to topple empires
and worlds and men.
In the catalytic movement
of the word, the world's heart beats,
years are gifted
and man's future secured.

It is all we have.

ELOQUENCE

A sigh escapes
the sealed lips,
betraying the apparent
tranquillity of the soul.
Gestures and cries
articulate the soul's distress,
unacknowledged.

Responding to
the soul's discontent,
the heart transmutes
in silence,
anguished breath
which heaven receives
to return in time,
exultant.

More eloquent than
the best turned phrase,
the sigh speaks volumes...
enamored itself
by returning love,
the sigh transposed,

becomes a song of joy.

THE POET'S MEMORIES

Torn from an event
with memories still alive
and placed in an incubator to breathe,
are poets expected to live.

Leaving a world incomplete,
they wander in vegetation
totally unfamiliar
and yet expected to survive.

And give rise to credence
in a world with no root,
where trees are shades
of others more vivid,
whose flowers whisper their names
in a forgotten language,
whose people are ghosts of livelier images,
all crowding the nimbus.

Where horizons are vast
and what eyes behold are stark lines
dividing two dimensional realities
pretending a depth that fools not a one.
Where snow sheds its stars
on a crystal night and the night becomes
a holy night eliciting unexpected
extravagances bestowing grace.

All grasped in a moment's vision
to linger through worlds creating ulcers
by gnawing the viscera
with dreams not completed.

The poet's pen
translates worlds of mean existence
from memories held
long in the heart's pocket.
Translates the colors of those other places
where winds caressed and sun bathed
a skin unlike his own.
In another place and time he walks
and because he does

his memories give rise to an Other's dream.

BEGINNINGS

We began
in universal waters
as particles of nonsense,
showing no discernment.
We collided and combusted
when two immutable pieces united.
We formed an eye of calm
in the maelstrom and grew.
Spongy surfaces
clung to us
and weedlike trails
spun from us.

With no conscious knowledge
we grew and yielded a vitrium
that put forth ague.

Our disposition
was entrusted
to a holier source than we.
For as we spun our sugars,
an Other spun for us.

In collusion,
we engendered knowledge
fraught with growing pains.
Our positions were tortured
by a history of emotions
and tattered memories, surfacing.
We danced on hot rocks.
We slept in cold places.
We loved in silence and cried out loud.
We became Man when we dreamed
the earth into being.

Even now we dream
of universal glory,
charting the voyage
through universal seas.
We will become a particle
in an Other's dream

whose discernment only now begins.

TRACKS

Check on that for me
and find out whether the tracks
are a rabbit's tracks.
See if in the new snow
they lead under the porch.

It has been such an old house
for so long,
even, I think,
when it was first built.
It has seen
with eyes blinking rapidly,
so many goings and comings.

Even with carpeted floors,
the goings and comings
are loudly announced
by creaking floors that shout,
'I am home! I am alive! I am here!'

The aware heart needs
no tracks in new snow
to know when love marches

through an old house.

MOON MEETING

You have emerged
from behind the trees.
If I should run my hand
across your face,
it would slide,
slick as a glossy magazine.

But I know as I near
and the night envelops me,
walking and running
through mist that upholds me,
I would halt beside you
for you would bar me further.

I would find myself
at the foot of the craggy mountain
chiseled from a distance,
like a cheekbone.
I thought I could smooth it
with a touch.

The eyes that have watched me
are deep pools
forcing me to swim depths
I shudder at.
But to reach the mind I know,
I would.

I would make me smooth as silk
to impress you
but my head is not yours.
So instead I stand the distance
to admire the beauty
that is you.

Luminescent white diamond
in the night,
knowing I too,
am watched by you.
How do I know?

The wanderer always finds his way home.

GENETIC MEMORIES

Lurking behind every door are ghosts
from a shadowy past,
eager to be translated
to a dubious present.

Impregnated in genes
are the memories of these ghosts,
split second DNA, with desire housing
the delicate substance quoting life.

Stupid am I to allow
others' memories,
lurking in my fresh Being,
to suck life out of my present.
But power filled, even to think
that I could release their tenacious hold
from a life unfulfilled
and requiring recompense.

Helplessness rages simultaneously,
pleading a judicious balance
to satisfy life's imbalances,
yet knowing,

I cannot do it.

NIGHT LIFE

I chase the last vestiges
of sleep from my eyes
and stretch my bones
as they click click like castanets
and happily resume their places.

The moon orchestrates
the room's shadows.
Hundreds of ghosted players
are ready to sound their A's.

The full symphony inspired
by the musical accompaniment
of the night sounds, begins.

The wood winds play
their eerie pursuit of
capturing the real wind.
The momentary silence invites the brass
to mimic the verbal cicadas.
The violins andante
follows the autos in movement
on the distant highway
and the concert beneath the stars
knows no end.

A cacophony of splendid noise,
a chalice readying to lift
even as the clock strikes.
The deep night yields
an anonymity to the thief stealing

a few more hours from the day's allotment.

THE NIGHT POEM

The day's frenzied cacophony
yields to the stilly night
its earned place.
Bedded in velvet, cushioned,
it hangs suspended.

Footsteps, now muffled, now sharp,
grant to their owner wings,
covering distances undreamed
in the moonless day.

Sharply defining shadows
playing cat and mouse,
rock the imagination
with apprehension.

Coverlet for the night
is the sky, perforated
by a million stars
too bright to will death.

Within,
the noiseless chatter ceases
in insipid gradations,
halting for an hour
the deepest dream.

Unbridled by night,
the heart endeavors to rehearse
with mind its elected course.
Pursuing now the greater awakening,
in sleep unencumbered,
the heart is pierced by night

to find life's blood replaced.

REFUGE IN DREAMS

In the beginning
when I was young
and when I was very cold,
I took my mammoth skin
and drew it closer about me
and found refuge in dreams.

Like a tourniquet
it stopped the flow of life
out of me.

Now I am old
and I huddle
still deeper in my woolen wrap.
Closing my eyes,
I discover refuge again in my dreams.
And find it stops

the flow of life out of me. Again.

SOMETIMES

There are memories
    in my pocket.
I carry them like folded linen
    and when needed,
I draw them forth to wipe my eyes.

Sometimes
    they are not used.
Sometimes in the morning
    I can take the memories
still neatly folded
    and carry them for another day,
unlaundered and unused.

It is amazing.
    Some people's memories
are unsightly.
    They are wrinkled
and soiled
    and all balled up.
They need laundering sometimes,
    after just one use.
Why, I wonder,
    are my memories now

so neat and clean?

THE SOUND CARRIES

I heard a heart break
and the sound
carried
throughout the house.

The crystal was struck,
the glass shattered
and the shards scattered
on the floor.

I did not know
a breaking heart
could cause such noise.
I could not pick up the pieces.

Would you?

TOWARD A DESTINY

wild geese move
within the moments of their destiny
framing patterns, struck
upon a naked sky.

clocked by indiscreet motions,
they move
in gentler waves
instinctively.

confirmed in their geesehood
they soar with speed
amid the chastening winds
and luring skies.

untethered, unfettered,
dressed in their celestial garb,
melding motive and design,

toward a destiny disclosed.

in a moment
they can do
what in a lifetime
I cannot.

THE HEALER

The storm clouds gather
and fear mounts,
harnessing power
which once were emotions
struggling for expression.

Like the great god Zeus,
brandishing his hot irons,
lightening arcs
across the night sky.

Thunder, like rolling kegs of dynamite,
flatten systems of tarnished beliefs,
leaving in its wake,
profound silence.

Forgotten are the thoughts
heavy with the weight of worry,
heavy with the futility
of life lived with no hope.

In her great capacity to heal,
Nature combines with man's emotions
to leave in her wake
renewed purpose,

if only to get things back to abnormal.

THE AUTUMN NIGHT

The velvet night plays host
to the September moon
hanging in suspension in liquid air.
Cold, crisp edges
seal in the lunar landscape,
forgetting for the moment,
the hot sky which sealed our noon.

There comes the night,
in desperation, relieving
the cloddish insensitivity visible
in the unrelenting stubbornness of the day,
unable and unwilling to release itself.

With relief,
the jagged beginning of the moon,
just now visible to the naked eye
makes its way across the horizon
of the mental landscape.

Its ridges,
its volcanic valleys split in two
and on the other side of the mind
it falls into the sun to rise
from flames on another night.

Having healed with mystic splendor,
balm for the day's wounds, it rests.
I drink in the day and forget.

But the night… the night ….
now bedded in honor, its place undisputed,
finds my words of gratitude hallow the ground

in worlds unattended.

EXIT

I am going
to jump out of who I am
and leap into the life
of who I will be.

I pray that
I will not have to
run back
and tie up loose ends again.

I am very tired
of running back
to where I was
and tired

of running on ahead
to prepare myself
for Me.

It is all a body can do for Now.

THE FINAL GESTURE

Tell me what you
want to hear
and I will say it.

But do not
ask me what I think
for I will tell you.

The time for play,
for games has passed
and already written legibly

are the words
no eye intent upon seeing
will miss,

or ears
intent upon hearing
will fail to hear.

Riddles plague us,
confusing, diluting,
to allow the throat to swallow

what the mind
cannot masticate.
Playthings, toys abound

and crowd the issues,
pressing us for attention.
At once the lessons

driven home seem hard to bear,
but with the arms up-thrust
in desperation,

the final gesture lifts man up.

MEMORY QUILT

When it is time
I will draw high
my memory quilt,
to cover shivering bones.

Pictured will be events
richly patterned
and pleasing
to the soul.

Astonishing not to recall
emotions pressed beyond belief,
battles fought
to frightful finishes.

Left like barnacles
clinging to a disabled craft,
slippery in substance,
suitable only for discard.

When it is time,
the memory quilt drawn
will show kaleidoscoped events
lending warmth to fragile skin,

haunting in their beauty
remembered,
while I take flight

in triumph, warmed.

IN THE MORNING

Today is the day
I will preen my feathers,
open my wings and fly.

Today is the day
I will breathe the elixir
of rarefied air

and bring to me
All That Is
into a heart grown weary.

And then I will find
the power to change
the course of mighty rivers

and give impetus
to dreaming children
who are content to sleepwalk.

In all this,
I will find the
crystalline gestures exquisite.

And dawn will break the crystals
and the children
will pick them up

astonished.

WHEN DAVID DIED

I say that David took the hands off my clocks. It was the greatest gift he could give me. I tire of running my life with a large hand and a small hand. No time for this, hurry for that. Do this now, do that before. I hate it. With a passion.

I want to immerse myself in time and swim in it. Feel it around me yielding and yet holding me up. I want to feel the eternity of it and I want to see my house and yard at different times under the sunTo be able to say that in the morning this is precisely how they look. I want the information stored in my Memory Bank for those times when I feel bereft.

I want to see the moon rise and give way to the sun. I want to see the rainbow around the moon and say again, we are in for a big snow. I need to revel in the mundane task of shaking out the kitchen rugs on the back porch and feel the cold boards beneath my slippers and the cold air stealing beneath my clothes. I want to keep looking at the moon with a glance, because no farmer stares at the moon too long and say hello David.

And when I feel very homesick, I will again as I have in the past, take my coffee out on the porch and sit beneath the midnight sky with the stars daring me to look up and identify them and again revel in this

multifaceted existence called Life.

HER TEACHERS

. . . .SPEAK .....

DID YOU SEE? DID YOU SEE?

I hung the moon
by its tail
from the nearest star
streaking across the sky
just for you.

Just for you I did it.

The moon argues for
the rights of the sun,
negotiated for the
rights of the day
and because the argument was just,
I granted it its place
and hung it from the nearest star
to be watchdog for the night.

Like a faithful pendulum
the moon stands the watch for you.

And if you can see its tail,
grasp it and swing on it.
It will negotiate
the rights of the world for you.
I will know then
that your eyes are

the eyes that see.

BLOOD RUN DRY

Peel back the linen shroud
which covers the bones of man
lying too long on his back.

Pull him to his feet
to stand long enough
to let the calluses form
to show him who he is.

You know too well
the day's events move
too slowly to take action.
Cobwebs lace his brain
and man's decisions at best
are obscure.

But wait, I speak.
And hold the chalice
to man's lips and watch him
drain it dry.
Such thirst cannot be satiated
by blood run dry.

I fed the hungry
with the food of my mouth,
but it goes undigested.
Instead I watch you
placating the placid
with the oil of words
soothing their wounds.

How long, I ask,
will you take the watch?
I see you

kiss the moon and bleed to death.

TO SAFE HARBOR AND WAIT

If I could take your hand
and point you in the right direction;
if I could take your thought
and turn it slightly to catch
the glint of the morning sun;
if I could take your sight
and set your eyes to catch
the shimmer of the coming moon
and if I could show you
where your heart belongs,
would I?

I would not.
For in your doing,
you find within yourself
hues to match the vibrancy
of the rising sun.
You find within
the core of the fruit,
seeds to start other worlds
and suns to circle them.

The sun dismisses itself from one world
to take precedence in another.
You sample these worlds,
deciding upon yours,
negotiating rock bound narrows
and cautiously maneuvering the straits.
But you do it.

And in the event of fog filled days,
seek safe harbor and wait.

For the fog also rises.

THE INSOMNIAC

You walk the night,
confined within the structure of your skull.
You pace, covering events that happen
in the time of your choosing,
gathering information from a past
that has lingered long past its prime,
subjecting both the event and its participator
to a scrutiny long envied
by the detailing historian.

You rise, no longer able to comfort
the body which is alternately,
hot and cold and at nines, not able to find
its niche in a century specifically designed for it.

The hands of the clock move imperceptibly
and the night has halted where you are,
trapping you within its black folds of skin,
waiting for you to peel back the dawn.

The world is a solitary confinement.
There is no better place to harbor the trysting soul
in search of its illusive lover, undeniably housed
in the half of civilization which sleeps.
Except for you. You pull the bathrobe
over shivering bones and light the lights
to mark your path to areas outside the perimeters
of your bed, seeking release from ghosts
whose grip you cling to.

Protesting vehemently all the while
your need for sleep, the mind in question
is reluctant to relinquish the day's
known infamies and yield trustingly
to the night's unknown.

There is surety, we think, in the knowledge
of our part in this day past.
We cannot be certain
this will be true of the night, or even if

we will wake to tell of it.

SPLITTING INFINITY

There is a space
layered between minutes
where our lives are lived
in a dimension of no time,
where air hangs heavy.

Filtering through the psyche
are bits and pieces of this reality.
With great weight it nudges
the paranoia of placidity,
inertia born of long standing.

Hammering into our consciousness
is the voice demanding its own.
Uneven, unequal to the present tense,
its thrust is felt, still.
Sliding between waves
of the persona's absence,
it yearns for recognition.

With a gesture you dismiss
the validity of what you are.
You hang the identity
of who you are on an illusion.
You grant to imagination
the word heard out of mind's context,
feelings unidentified,
on a bloated stomach.

Fear paralyzes,
plunging the pilgrim
into a grim state of no confrontation.
Fragments and shards
of other worlds pierce your shields,
unrelentedly.

It is with precision
the arrow which lodges in the heart
finds the path

must first splinter the mind.

WHITE STONE

I will give you a white stone.
        On the stone will be your name
and you will read it and remember it.
        I have called you over and over
so you would not forget it.

I have loved you long before the earth was,
        even before we first walked the heavens.
I have shown you how to love,
        unconditionally and forever.

I have been generous with your love.
        I have spread it profusely
and the earth greens.
        I have sprinkled it finely
and with long fingers,
        I have pressed your love into the heavens
and you call them stars.

I have taken the heat of your love
        and put it all together
to warm the earth and you call it Sun.

I have stood you on a hot rock
        and you molded it
into a cool sphere and I took it proudly
        and set it to light the night sky
and we call it Moon and man loves by it.

The moon warms his passions
        when they flag
and the sun browns his body
        when it pales
and the green earth eases
        when the rocks pierce his feet.

But the stars are for you,
        for you counted them and found
the heavens could not hold all of them,

        so I put the remainder in man's eyes.

FOR NOW...

Let your mind answer
your heart's murmuring,
for in the sanctity
of self,
you will see your divinity.

In the august crucible
that is Earth,
latticed by clouds
hovering the trees,
you gain your peace.

In the musing
of the grass growing
to reach its height
and to color
the bare earth
with a piled carpet,
you feel the hallowed crest.

In all,
gently tend the heart's rending
and choose the teachers
who match the performance

of your innate goodness.